YAJURVEDA IN A NUTSHELL

DR. JAGADEESH PILLAI

Made with ♥ on the Notion Press Platform
www.notionpress.com

Dedicated to all those who are keen of sharpening their wisdom

Contents

Contents

Prayer

Om Bhadram Karnnebhih Shrnnuyaama Devaah |

Bhadram Pashyema-Akssabhir-Yajatraah |

Sthirair-Anggais-Tussttuvaamsas-Tanuubhih |

Vyashema Devahitam Yad-Aayuh |

Svasti Na Indro Vrddha-Shravaah |

Svasti Nah Puussaa Vishva-Vedaah |

Svasti Nas-Taakssaryo Arisstta-Nemih |

Svasti No Vrhaspatir-Dadhaatu ||

Om Shaantih Shaantih Shaantih ||

About The Author

Dr. Jagadeesh Pillai four times Guinness World Record holder, a voracious reader, writer, and true research scholar was born in Varanasi, the abode of Lord Shiva. He is Ph.D. in Vedic Science. He is a multi-faceted polymath with innate qualities, creative ideas and many remarkable achievements. Although his roots extend back to "Gods own Country"(Kerala), the residents of Varanasi feel proud of him and adore him as a child of Varanasi who caters to every individual in need without any expectations. A deep study into his profile reflects that he has added so many feathers to his cap which makes him quite unique. He is a four times Guinness Book of World Records Holder in the following subjects :

1. "Script to Screen" which he achieved by producing and directing a state of art animation film within the shortest time possible by breaking the earlier set record by Canadians. There are many national and international Awards and Recognitions to his credit.

2. Longest Line of Post Cards which he has done on the occasion of 163 years of Indian Postal Day by 16300 post cards. The event was also connected with a questionnaire about Indian Flag.

3. Largest Poster Awareness Campaign – This was achieved by designing an awareness campaign on the subject "Beti Bachao – Beti Padhao".

4. Largest Envelop – Towards tribute to Prime Minister's

initiative 'Make in India' – he has created about 4000 sq meter envelop using waste papers.

5. Attempted by lighting 70000 candles on a 210 kg cake to celebrate the 70th Indian Independence day recorded in World Records India.

6. Attempted a documentary on Dhamek Stupa of Sarnath dubbing in 17 languages, result is waiting from Guinness World Records.

He is versatile in Gita teaching. The young generation is fond of his Gita teaching and he has changed the life of many young through his continued motivational boost up and teachings.

He has composed and sung Gayatri Mantra in 1008 different tunes.

He has composed and sung Hanuman Chalisa in 108 different tunes.

He has composed and sung hundreds of Sanskrit Bhajans, Patriotic songs, etc.

He has written and directed so many short films and documentaries for awareness campaigns.

He has done voluntary services to UP Police and Kerala Police to spread awareness campaigns on the various issue through videos and photography.

He is on the path of authoring thousands of books on Indian culture, Indian Temples, and the life of extraordinary people.

It is hard to believe that he has produced and directed more than 100 Documentaries on a particular city (Varanasi) which is done by a single person.

He has helped and guided more than 25 boys and girls to achieve world records through various creative and innovative methods.

A multifaceted person who can apply the best of his intellect using the God-given blessings which have been showered upon every human being granting them an immense capacity to learn, experience, and experiment with many things and do wonders in this world of discrimination and disparities.

He is a teacher and a student at the same time who always learns every day and teaches every day. As a master, his weakness was that he never sticks to a particular subject. Perhaps this weakness gives him the strength to master any area which he came across.

Each of his days dawned with learning a new topic and he spend most of his time experimenting and researching it.

He is also a selfless social activist and a motivational speaker.

His life was full of struggle, ups and downs, and failures.

But he never gave up and faced all his trials and tribulations full of confidence. Today he is a successful young man with a lot of enthusiasm and rich life experience.

He has sung full Ram Charita Manas 51 hours audio by his own composition. He has also sung the whole Bhagavad-Gita in his own composition with a rhythmic background.

He has also sung "Lokah Samastha Sukhino Bhavantu" in 50 different languages.

Currently working on a detailed and scientific study on Veda, Upanishad, Puranas, Bhagavad Gita, etc.

He has composed and sung Hanuman Chalisa in 108 different compositions and Gayatri Mantra in 1008 different compositions.

Awards

Four Times Guinness World Records

Winner of Mahatma Gandhi Vishwa Shanti Puraskar

Mahatma Gandhi Global Peace Ambassador

Kashi Ratna Award

Dr. APJ Abdul Kalam Motivational Person of the Year 2017

Mother Teresa Award

Indira Gandhi Priyadarshini Award

Bharat Vikas Ratna Award

Udyog Ratna Award

Vigyan Prasar Award

Poorvanchal Ratn Samman

Preface

Yajurveda is one of the four ancient scriptures of Hinduism. It mainly deals with the rituals related to sacrifices and is said to be written in an archaic form of Sanskrit. The core of Yajurveda consists mostly of hymns addressed to various deities, prayers, and mantras for use in ritualistic offerings. These mantras address themes such as social welfare, protection from evil forces, and empower individuals through divine powers. In addition, it also contains a wide array of philosophical teachings about morality and ethics. The Yajurveda covers topics such as Sacrificial rituals and ceremonies, Dharma (moral laws), Nature Worship, Purity rites, as well as invocations for peace and serenity. All this against the backdrop of Vedic literature which serves to bring musicianship into India's spiritual life!

This book provides a straightforward understanding of the contents of the Yajurveda, the importance of its verses, and the wisdom they impart. It is an invaluable resource for anyone seeking to gain insight into this ancient text and its teachings. By exploring the Yajurveda, readers can gain a deeper understanding of the spiritual and philosophical foundations of Hinduism and its timeless relevance to modern life.

Preface

CHAPTER ONE

Yajurveda - Introduction

Yajurveda is one of the four sacred texts of Hinduism, and contains a vast collection of Vedic knowledge, spiritual and religious teachings. The other three being the Rigveda, Atharvaveda, and Smriti. Yajurveda is composed of white and black verses, or suktas, whichare divided into four sections, or Khandas. It contains rituals, prayers, and hymns that are used in religious worship ceremonies related to an individual.

Yajurveda is mainly focused on explaining the technical aspects of Vedic sacrifices and also contains a significant amount of theological passages, philosophy, cosmology and mythology. The rituals described in the text were used to invoke various gods, who were expected to bless human beings with wealth and prosperity. It was believed that the performance of such rituals and hymns, along with offering of oblations, was essential for the attainment of physical, mental, and spiritual well-being.

Yajurveda is also known for its philosophy of karma and the resultant concept of rebirth. It teaches that the soul has aeternal existence and its life is affected not just by its present deeds, but also by its past actions. According to the text, karma or the consequences of deeds must be borne either in the present or other succeeding births. It is believed that the soul pays for positive deeds with greater rewards such as happiness, wealth, peace and prosperity, while negative actions result in suffering, bondage, and unhappiness.

Yajurveda is also considered to be an important source of knowledge about ancient Hinduism and its religious practices. It provides a strong basis for studying the role of Vedic deities, their relationships with human beings, and the rituals associated with them. It was believed to be the most important book in ancient India, before the advent of modern religious texts, as it served as a guide for performing rituals and prayers.

Yajurveda is an integral aspect of Hinduism as it explains the importance of Vedic sacrifices and the connection between human beings and their gods. It is a source of spiritual knowledge, guidance and instruction on how to attain material, mental and spiritual well-being. Additionally, it explains the power of karma and the cyclical nature of existence, and the importance of performing rituals in order to obtain blessings and prosperity. All of this combined makes Yajurveda an essential part of Hinduism and its traditions.

CHAPTER TWO

VERSES OF YAJURVEDA

The Yajur Veda is one of the four sacred texts, or Vedas, that form the spiritual foundation of Hinduism. This ancient text contains verses for ceremonial rituals that have been used for thousands of years in India. Yajur Veda, meaning "Knowledge of Sacrifice", is an important source of spiritual and ritual knowledge in Hinduism.

The Yajur Veda consists of verses or mantras that are used in ritualistic ceremonies, such as worship of a deity or sacrifice, and have been used since the very early periods of Hinduism. These verses are typically chanted or recited by a priest, who will also provide guidance to the participants throughout the ceremony. The Yajur Veda includes verses related to various deities and themes, such as the power of karma, divine protection and the cycle of death and rebirth.

The importance of Yajur Veda verses in Hindu rituals is undeniable. These sacred texts provide both an avenue for communication with the divine, and a way to create a shared spiritual experience for those participating in the ceremony. Yajur Veda verses are believed to not only bring blessings to those participating in a ritual, but also serve as an invocation to the gods for assistance and protection. For example, a verse may be used to ask for divine guidance in the form of a boon from a deity.

Yajur Veda verses are also important in traditional Hindu ceremonies, such as the Hindu wedding ceremony. During the wedding ritual, the couple exchanges ritualistic vows and a priest recites verses from the Yajur Veda as a way of honoring the Divine. This is believed to bring good fortune to the couple as they begin their new life together. Moreover, it also serves as a reminder to the couple that their union is protected and blessed by the Divine.

In many ways, the Yajur Veda is integral to Hinduism. It provides an important source of wisdom and spiritual guidance, as well as a gateway into the divine realm. The verses contained in the Yajur Veda offer insight into the deeper mysteries of life, and serve as a powerful tool for ritualistic invocation. By understanding and respecting its importance, we can become better connected to the spiritual fabric of Hinduism.

CHAPTER THREE

RISHIES OF YAJURVEDA

The Yajurveda is one of the four Vedas and is notable for its rituals, hymns and philosophies. Yajurveda is considered to be the oldest of the four Vedas and is the foundation on which many Hindu doctrines are based. It is also an important source for understanding ancient Hindu customs and beliefs. One of the most prominent figures in the Yajurveda is that of the Rishies, or Rishis.

Rishies are believed to have been spiritual teachers or seers who are said to have been revealed knowledge directly from the gods. Their teachings form the basis of the Yajurveda and their ideas have heavily influenced the Vedic period of Indian culture. The Rishies were responsible for codifying the ancient wisdom and spiritual knowledge of the Vedic texts. They were also known for their astrological and astronomical findings, such as calculating planetary positions, observing eclipses and cataloguing the movements of the sun, moon and planets.

In Vedic literature, the Rishies are portrayed as gods, sages and wise men who were sent down to teach mankind. They were renowned for their morals, spiritual capabilities and wisdom. They were seen as respected representatives of the gods who could provide teachings, advice and guidance to the people. Many of their teachings are still used in modern Hinduism.

Perhaps most importantly, the Rishies can be credited with creating and promoting a vibrant culture of hymn-singing and religious rites within the Vedic tradition. The hymns composed by the Rishies are considered to be some of the oldest literary works of Hinduism, and they have been used for centuries in Hindu ceremonies. In modern times, these hymns are still sung in Hindu rituals, such as weddings and religious festivals.

In conclusion, the Rishies of the Yajurveda were revered spiritual figures who had a great influence on ancient Hindu culture. They laid the foundations of Vedic religion and culture by compiling the wisdom of the gods and putting it into written form. The hymns and rituals created by the Rishies still play an important role in Hinduism today.

CHAPTER FOUR

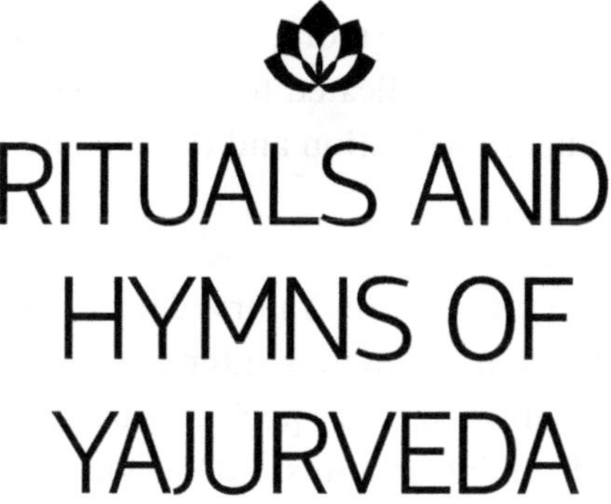

RITUALS AND HYMNS OF YAJURVEDA

Yajurveda is a sacred text of the Vedic religion which, together with the four other books, of which it is composed, comprise over a thousand hymns of various devotional and ritualistic applications. These hymns and rituals have been traditional practices of Hinduism for centuries and today, Yajurveda remains an important source of spiritual knowledge, especially among the educated elites of the Indian society.

The Yajurveda contains numerous hymns which promote the performance of various spiritual ceremonies and actions. These hymns are divided into three distinct categories: deva yajna, for worshiping the Gods, pitryajna for honoring ancestors, and adhyanam, for meditating and studying spirituality and religion.

Each category contains specific rituals and hymns to be performed and chanted. The deva yajna includes rituals such as Agni (fire ritual), Ganapati (worshiping and honoring the Hindu God, Ganesha) and Rudra (worshiping the God of storms, Rudra) and these are accompanied by specific hymns. Furthermore, the pitryajna includes prayers and offerings dedicated to the ancestors, while the adhyanam includes meditation and the recitation of sacred incantations.

Another important part of Yajurveda are the Samhitas. These are collections of hymns intended to be chanted in a particular order as part of specific rituals. For example, the Rig Veda Samhita contains 1,028 hymns meant to be recited as part of a ritualistic offering of rituals to the deity Agni. The Yajur Veda Samhita, on the other hand, contains a series of hymns devoted to several Vedic Gods, including the Caturvarna Samhita, dedicated to the four main classes of society, and the Pranagnihotra Samhita, devoted to the gods of nature.

Yajurveda also provides insight into the importance of self-discipline and virtuous living, both of which are necessary in order to attain liberation (Moksha) and gain access to Brahman, the ultimate spiritual reality. As such, it is believed that the Yajurveda is able to provide guidance in the quest for spiritual enlightenment.

In conclusion, the sacred texts of Yajurveda provide us with an invaluable source of insight into the spiritual practices of Hinduism. Through its hymns and rituals, it is able to provide guidance in the quest for spiritual knowledge and liberation and provide an invaluable source of insight into the importance of self-discipline and virtuous living.

CHAPTER FIVE

YAJURVED BRAHMANAS AND MANTRA CHANTING

The Yajurved Brahmans are a type of Hindu priests associated with the chanting of mantras and the practice of Hinduism. They are considered to be the most ancient of the four priestly classes of Vedic India. The Yajurved Brahmans are believed to have been in existence for about five thousand years and have an important role in the rituals and practices of Hinduism.

The Yajurved Brahmans are responsible for chanting the numerous mantras, or sacred formulas, during religious ceremonies. These mantras are chanted in a vibrational manner, with a specific tone and cadence depending on the type of ceremony being performed. The chanted mantras are believed to invoke the presence of the gods and goddesses, who take part in the ritual. The ritual can also involve invocations to the ancestors, religious figures, and other spiritual entities. The chanting of the mantras is meant to provide protection, guidance, and prosperity to the participants of the ritual.

Mantras come in many forms, including hymns and chants, as well as recitations of hymnals and scriptures. The Yajurved Brahmans are also responsible for chanting these mantras and rituals at specific times, depending on the beliefs and customs of the people involved.

The Yajurved Brahmans chant mantras in a particular way, with a specific intonation and rhythm. This rhythmic chanting helps to create an atmosphere and vibration that engages the gods and goddesses and helps to bring forth their blessings. In addition to producing a sacred vibration, the chanting of mantras also has psychological and spiritual benefits. After chanting a mantra, the devotee typically experiences a feeling of inner peace, self-actualization, and joy.

The Yajurved Brahmans are essential in the practice of Hinduism. Their unwavering devotion to Hinduism is reflected in their dedication to the chanting of mantras, and their rituals and customs have been passed down for generations. Their involvement has provided centuries of guidance, protection, and prosperity to believers of the faith.

CHAPTER SIX

DEVATAS IN YAJURVEDA

Yajurveda is an ancient Indian scripture which forms part of the four canonical sacred texts known as the Vedas. It is composed of mantras that were revealed to ancient sages. An important part of this scripture is the worship of divinities or devatas.

The devatas of the Yajurveda hold a very significant place in the Hindu religion. They are the objects of worship and are believed to bestow blessings upon their devotees. Devatas are said to represent abstract cosmic forces such as the sun, wind, fire, and thunder. Thus, worshipping them is said to bring about harmony in nature and the universe.

The Yajurveda devatas are divided into three types: celestial, terrestrial, and atmospheric. Each type has its own set of devatas and each has a different significance. Celestial devatas, for example, are associated with the heavenly planets and include the sun, moon, stars, and deities such as Indra, Agni, and Varuna. Terrestrial devatas are linked to the Earth and include Prithvi, Varuna, and Parjanya. Atmospheric devatas, finally, pertain to forces present in the atmosphere such as Vastospati, Marut, and Rudra. Each of these devatas has its own significance and is viewed as a symbol of a particular cosmic force.

The devatas of the Yajurveda are very important in Hinduism, as they are the focus of ritualistic worship. Prayers and chanting of mantras in their names is believed to please them and seek their blessings. Devatas are also seen as the protectors and controllers of the universe, ensuring peace and harmony. By worshipping them, one seeks harmony between nature and cosmic forces.

The worship of the devatas of the Yajurveda is still practiced in present times and continues to play an important role in the lives of Hindus. Thus, the devatas of the Yajurveda are significant in the Hindu religion and culture, symbolizing powerful cosmic forces and their worship being believed to provide the harmonious balance that is essential for living a meaningful life.

CHAPTER SEVEN

YAJURVEDA MANTRA FOR DAY TO DAY LIFE

The Yajurveda is one of the four Vedas, which are the oldest religious texts in the world, and hold a special status among Hindus throughout India. As the name suggests, the Yajurveda is mainly associated with yajna (sacrifice or worship). It includes the mantras and practices that are fundamental to how we understand Hinduism and the daily practice of religious rituals and practices in the lives of devotees.

The Yajurveda Mantra for Day To Day Life holds great significance for Hindus and is steeped in mythology. It is said that the mantras are derived from the gods themselves and can be used to guide and support people in facing life's obstacles and thriving in their spiritual journey. This set of Sanskrit hymns can be found within the Yajurveda, the third Veda of the four Vedas known as the 'Whole Knowledge'.

One of the most common Yajurveda mantras is the "gayatri mantra". This mantra is a prayer to the sun god, asking for protection and guidance in difficult times. The mantra is chanted every morning by devotees in order to maintain peace, purity and harmony. This mantra helps them to remind themselves of their divine purpose and to remain humble and devoted to their faith.

The Yajurveda offers many other mantras, all with their own unique messages and meanings. For example, one mantra is called the "Bhadrakali mantram". This is a powerful mantra for protection and aids in removing any negative energy that might be surrounding a person or a space. The mantra is mainly used for overcoming fear or anxiety, and is often recited during times of turmoil or conflict.

Another Yajurveda mantra is the "Om Trambakam Yajamahe" mantra. This mantra is said to bring peace and happiness in the life of its reciter, as well as fullness and prosperity. It is said to also bring harmony and compassion in relationships, and is a reminder to devotees to always seek truth and to remain devoted to their faith.

The Yajurveda mantras and teachings have been passed down through generations and are still an important part of Hindu religion and culture. It is a source of knowledge, strength, and courage and provides us with a spiritual framework and connection to our past. The mantras can provide us with solace in times of sorrow and comfort in times of despair. They also help us to focus on our daily spiritual practices and to remain mindful throughout our day to day lives.

CHAPTER EIGHT

MODERN APPROACH TO YAJURVEDA

The modern approach to Yajurveda, one of the four ancient Hindu scriptures collectively known as the Vedas, is rooted in the spiritual, religious and philosophical teachings of the Vedas and their interconnectedness with the physical world. Yajurveda is traditionally associated with the knowledge of rituals, sacrifices, and fire ceremonies, but today there's an effort to interpret it in the context of modern life. The modern approach to Yajurveda seeks to draw on its traditional roots while also considering new evidence and insights that can provide creative interpretations to the scriptures.

At the foundation of the modern approach to Yajurveda is a deep respect for the traditional teachings and interpretations that have been passed down through the ages. This includes an understanding of the deep connections between religion, spirituality and the physical world, something that has been highlighted in many ancient Vedic texts. By incorporating this traditional understanding of Yajurveda, scholars and individuals can uncover meanings and insights that help create harmony between the physical and spiritual worlds.

The modern approach to Yajurveda also includes an understanding of modern science and technology. By synthesizing the wisdom of the Vedas with scientific knowledge and evidence, scholars can draw on both to gain a better understanding of the spiritual concepts found in Yajurveda. By exploring the physical world, scholars can further enhance the spiritual understanding of Yajurveda by interpreting it in a modern context.

The modern approach to Yajurveda has also become a tool for promoting the harmonization of religious and spiritual concepts between different traditions. In particular, the modern approach to Yajurveda often highlights the similarities between Hinduism and other religions. This helps bridge religious divides and create dialogue between different traditions, allowing for a more unified world view.

At its core, the modern approach to Yajurveda seeks to stay true to the Vedic teachings while also embracing innovation. By taking an integrated approach, scholars can access deeper insight into both the spiritual and physical aspects of the scriptures. Ultimately, it is the modern approach to Yajurveda that helps individuals come to a greater understanding of their world, one that stays true to the traditions of the past while also staying current with modern life.

CHAPTER NINE

YAJURVEDA AND UPANISHAD

The Yajurveda and the Upanishad together form the holiest of Hindu scriptures and together constitute the Veda. The Yajurveda is mostly a collection of sacrificial formulas and mantras, called Yajus, while the Upanishad form the supplementary part of the Veda and is a source of spiritual knowledge. It is known as Vedanta, the 'end of the Veda'.

The Yajurveda and the Upanishads are connected in an inseparable way and are the complementary parts of each other. On one hand, Yajurveda focuses on the karmic practices and rituals, while the Upanishads focus upon self-realization. The Upanishads serve to bridge the gap between the mundane rituals of the body and the attainment of Self-Realization. Both the texts are part of the eternal teaching of the Vedic tradition that leads to spiritual insight.

The Upanishads, which means sitting near, give the highest spiritual instructions to reach the ultimate goal of a Yogi, called Moksha, which is liberation from the cycle of birth, death and rebirth. As per the Upanishads, the ultimate goal of a Yogi is to realize Brahman, the Supreme Soul, which is beyond all dualities and distinctions. The Upanishads contain spiritual concepts, such as the cycle of actions, the will of God, and the concepts of Self-Realization, Brahman, and God.

The Yajurveda and the Upanishads are deeply interlinked and both contain the secrets to attaining Moksha. In his commentary on the Upanishads, Adi Shankaracharya points out, "The sacred Vedas are two in number: the Sukla Yajurveda and the Krishna Yajurveda. Both these sacred scriptures form the basis of Vedanta and elucidate the nitty-gritty of karma and Upasana, i.e., worship."

The Upanishads constitute the philosophical part of the Vedic texts, while the Yajurveda contains the mantras and chants used in ritualistic offerings and worship. The Upanishads expound upon the philosophical meanings of the mantras and chants which are the core components of the Yajurveda. Therefore, without one, the other cannot be properly understood and interpreted.

In conclusion, both the Yajurveda and the Upanishad are essential for attaining Moksha, or Self-Realization. They cannot be viewed separately, as both focus on different aspects of the Vedic teachings. The Yajurveda outlines the karmic practices of worship and prayer, while the Upanishads explain and interpret the philosophical concepts and theories related to it. Together, they form the core of the Vedic texts and are essential for achieving spiritual enlightenment.

CHAPTER TEN

YAJURVEDA AND BHAGAVAD GITA

The Bhagavad Gita is a revered Hindu scripture that captures the teachings of the Supreme Lord Krishna. It is comprised of 700 verses of which many are sourced from the Yajur Veda. As such, a close examination of their origins provides a great deal of insight into the relationship between the two scriptures.

It is important to understand that the Vedas are considered the most sacred and ancient scriptures of the Hindu tradition. They are regarded as revelation and are believed to have been revealed to sages and seers, who composed them and then transmitted them orally for several millennia until they were committed to writing around 1000 BCE. The Yajur Veda, in particular, is one of the four Vedic scriptures and contains the liturgy during sacrificial rituals.

The Bhagavad Gita, on the other hand, although believed to be over 5,000 years old, is only a small part of the larger Mahabharata epic. It is essentially an account of a discussion that unfolds between Lord Krishna and warrior-prince Arjuna on a battlefield, moments before the onset of a great war.

The Yajur Veda and Bhagavad Gita are intrinsically connected, insofar as many teachings in the Bhagavad Gita come from the Yajur Veda. One example can be found in Chapter 3, verse 35 of the Bhagavad Gita which states, "All actions take place in the mind and because of mental determination, they rub off on even an inert body". This sentiment is taken almost verbatim from the Yajur Veda's Chapter 4, verse 16.

Generally speaking, many of the teachings in the Bhagavad Gita are formulated with the ethos of karma and liberation, which are found in the Yajur Veda. To that end, the sacred scriptures of the Yajur Veda provide a broader context for the many allusions, symbols and analogies discussed throughout the Gita's 700 verses. As such, it is accurate to regard Yajur Veda and the Bhagavad Gita as closely related scriptures.

Overall, the Yajur Veda and the Bhagavad Gita are intrinsically and intricately connected. Not only does the Bhagavad Gita comprise the contents of the Yajur Veda in many instances, it also provides context and depth to the many teachings of the Veda. Furthermore, the Yajur Veda and Bhagavad Gita share many teachings and principles, particularly those related to karma and liberation. Taken together, they represent two closely related scriptures that remain central to the Hindu tradition.

CHAPTER ELEVEN

YAJURVEDA AND 18 PURANAS

Yajurveda, while being one of the four Vedas, has close ties to the eighteen puranas. The Vedas and the Puranas constitute the revelation of God's truth, quintessentially recognizing the same basic truths in different forms to be comprehended according to individual capacities. Both are dedicated to honoring God's characteristics and realities of existence, with Yajurveda for the purpose of establishing rituals, and the Puranas for providing knowledge about events, myths, wisdom and philosophy.

Yajurveda is considered the source for the eighteen Puranas, as the statutes of gods and godly activities mentioned in the Puranas are first found in the Yajurveda. Furthermore, Yajurveda is considered to be the essence of the Puranas, as the different methods of worship are based on the mantras and rituals that were originated by this Vedic scripture. Even the exact explanation of the Puranic stories found in Yajurveda direct the readers to the eighteenth Puranas. Throughout the Upanishads, Puranas, and epics, the details in the Yajurveda are visible, suggesting that the sages had committed it to the memory.

Moreover, the Yajurveda is seen as the source of many different sects and cults, which are based on different gods, with the mention of the eighteen Puranas being the only source to comprise of these sects. It investigates the features, powers, activities, and pastimes of various Deity forms, thus allowing for the proper comprehension and conclusion of prayer rituals. Yajurveda's verses provide each sect or school of practice and worship with proper instructions. This is why the sages have carefully and diligently described the Puranic activities in detail in the Yajurveda.

The Yajurveda and the eighteen Puranas are irrevocable evidence of ancient India's tendency of deity worship. Yajurveda lays the foundations for understanding about these sects and cults through its mantras and verses. Also, it not only provides the sacred rules and regulations for the establishment of rituals in families, but also with respect to deity worship, as it has been stated many times in the Puranas and Upanishads. The effort of the sages is highly commendable and acts as a guide to prayer rituals, as well as an essential reference book for the Puranas.

Summarily, it can be clearly seen that Yajurveda has a deep connection to the eighteen Puranas, both serving as sources for understanding deity lore, as well as providing a foundational basis for rituals, mantras and prayer worship. Without the Yajurveda, the Puranas would not have the prominent position and respect it has in the Indian traditions.

CHAPTER TWELVE

YAJURVEDA AND FIVE ELEMENTS

Yajurveda is one of the four ancient books compiled by ancient sages in India, collectively known as the Vedas. Yajurveda contains mantras and rituals related to the yajna, a Hindu sacrificial fire ritual. This Vedic scripture has two versions, the White Yajurveda and the Black Yajurveda. Yajurveda, dedicated to the Vedic god of fire Agni, teaches of the five elements in nature, their properties and how they are related to one another.

The five elements of nature, known as the "Pancha Mahabhutas", are akasha (space or ether), vayu (air), agni (fire), jala (water), and prithvi (earth). According to Yajurveda, these five elements are essential for various aspects of life and unifying these components with the act of yajna (sacrifice) helps to maintain a balance between the spiritual and natural world.

The element of akasha is the basis of all other elements. Akasha signifies both absence and space, and it is believed to pervade everywhere in creation. Akasha gives rise to other elements, allowing them to manifest in the material world and manifest in human life. Vayu, the wind element, is the aspect of akasha which allows for movement, growth and change in creation. Vayu also governs the breath, and is associated with the mind and nervous system.

The Agni element is the embodiment of energy. Using the fire element, one can transform and transmutate whatever is found in nature. Agni is the power behind transformation, and it's influence helps maintain the balance between the spiritual and physical realms. Jala, water element, is associated with mercy and compassion. Jala is necessary for all living things to survive and flourish. Prithvi, the earth element, provides support and stability and is integral to the material world. Prithvi is the element of stability.

Yajurveda recognizes the importance of applying the right energy at the right time. Through the rituals of yajna, the five elements are put together in balance and harmony, and their energies are tapped into for both spiritual and physical benefits and blessings. Yajurveda also teaches that these five elements should be revered and given proper respect. A worshipper who understands the connection between these five elements and the way in which their power works together can deepen their understanding of the spiritual and material worlds and achieve a greater spiritual connection.

The five elements of Yajurveda reach far beyond the physical realm and represent an important part of the ancient Vedic culture. Through these elements, yajna and the mantras of Yajurveda, practitioners can tap into the power of nature and gain insight and understanding into their own spiritual journey.

CHAPTER THIRTEEN

INTERNATIONAL AUTHORS COMMENTARIES ON YAJURVEDA

Yajurveda International Authors Commentaries is a large collection of books and journals on the study of the Vedas, an ancient Indian spiritual and religious texts. This collection encompasses the knowledge of Yajurveda, which is the scripture of the Hindu faith and its teachings, as well as commentaries of scholars from across the world. This extensive library offers an insight into the traditional approach of studying and understanding the Vedas, with specific commentaries on various topics such as Vedanta, esoteric symbolism and other related spiritual teachings. It includes works of famous Indian authors like Sri Aurobindo, Sri Ramakrishna, Swami Vivekananda, Mahatma Gandhi, Acharya Vinoba Bhave, Maharshi Mahesh Yogi, and numerous other authors both modern and ancient.

The authors' commentaries are divided into two categories: original and translated. The original commentaries are written by renowned authors in the Indian subcontinent. These include commentaries on all the four Vedas namely Rig Veda, Yajur Veda, Sama, and Atharva. The Yajurveda International Author's commentaries are based on traditional texts and structure, as well as original perspectives of the authors. The translations are of classical texts in Sanskrit, as well as essays and other works from authors in other countries and cultures, such as China, Japan, England, and other countries.

The library of Yajurveda International Author's Commentaries is designed to draw from the traditional Indian knowledge system, as well as the modern world's interpretation of the Vedas and its studies. This library consists of commentaries on a range of topics related to the spiritual and philosophical aspects of the Vedas and its related studies, that can be immensely useful to scholars, seekers and practitioners of Vedic knowledge.

Yajurveda International Author's Commentaries includes commentaries by classical authors such as Badarayana, Patanjali, Patañjali and Acharya Shankara. There are commentaries written by modern authors like Sri Aurobindo, Swami Kriyananda, Dr. Vamadeva Shastri, Dr. Natalia Isailovic and various others. The authors' commentaries provide a universal view of the Vedas, combining traditional Indian knowledge with modern interpretations.

Yajurveda International Author's Commentaries are an important part of the study and practice of the Vedas and its related knowledge and culture. Not only will it help deepen one's understanding of the Vedic philosophy, but it will also provide other scholars with insights from different perspectives.

CHAPTER FOURTEEN

INDIAN SCHOLARS COMMENTARIES ON YAJURVEDA

Yajurveda is one of four ancient scriptures of the Vedic religion. The text is divided into three major parts: The White Yajurveda (also known as Krishna Yajurveda, Taittiriya Samhita, etc.), Black Yajurveda (Shukla Yajurveda, Katha Samhita, etc.) and The Shatapatha Brahmana. Over the centuries, many great Indian scholars have contributed to the commentaries, translations and interpretations of Yajurveda.

Sayana (c. 1300 – c. 1388) was a Vedic scholar, statesman and philosopher from South India. He was the court-poet to four different ruling dynasties which helped him produce some remarkable translations, commentaries and works on philosophy. Sayana wrote two major commentaries (bhashya) on Yajurveda – one on White Yajurveda and the other on Black Yajurveda, in which he employed the use of elaborate language.

Vyasatirtha (1460–1539 CE) was a great scholar and the second inveterate of the philosophical institution at Udupi, part of the prominent Vaishnava monasteries or Matts of Karnataka. He was especially proficient in the study of White Yajurveda and his commentaries are most commonly referred to as the Yajurvidabhashyabhumika. He used the gau thva spoken style which incorporated Vedic rituals and ordered compositions in-line with the simple language of common people. His commentaries explain the traditional rites and the Upanishads, thus integrating the Vedic religion with philosophy.

Madhavacarya (1238–1317 CE), also known as Madhva, was one of the most important scholars of Yajurveda from the Dvaita school of philosophy. He wrote over thirty works including commentaries on Taittiriya Upanishad and Bhagvad Gita. He also wrote commentaries (bhashya) on Shatapatha Brahmana and White Yajurveda. Madhva was one of the first scholars to introduce the concept of "absolute monotheism" and emphasized on following the paths of God in spirit.

Govindppacarya (1483– 1561 CE), son of Vyasatirtha, was an influential scholar of Yajurveda from the Vadiraja Mutt in Udupi, Karnataka. He was the author of many commentaries on the Vedic scriptures and philosophical works. He wrote two important commentaries on Yajurveda – the Shatapatha Bhashya on Shatapatha Brahmana and the Vyasapramana Bhashya on the Krishna Yajurveda.

CHAPTER FIFTEEN

KRISHNA YAJURVEDA AND SHUKLA YAJURVEDA

The Yajurveda is one of the four primary ancient Hindu scriptures, consisting of both prose and mantra. The Yajurveda is divided into two distinct texts called the Krishna or "Black" Yajurveda and the Shukla or "White" Yajurveda. While both traditions share many common concepts and liturgies, they also present distinct beliefs and practises in Vedic ritual.

The major difference between the two traditions is primarily associated with the liturgical chants. The Krishna Yajurveda follows an oral tradition of chanting the Vedic mantras. This system is called the "Taittiriya Shakha" and primarily relies on the memorization of Vedic mantras by the priests who are part of the Yajurvedic order. The Shukla Yajurveda, on the other hand, follows a more traditional literary style of writing down the mantras on parchment paper. This method of recording is known as the

"Vājasaneyi-Samhitā" and is commonly referred to as the White Yajurveda.

In addition to these primary differences in the physical compositions of the Yajurvedas, there are also subtle variations in their ritual practises. For example, the ritual for the new-moon sacrifice is slightly different in the Krishna Yajurveda when compared to the Shukla Yajurveda. The primary differences here are related to the number of offerings and the sacred objects used in the ritual. Another difference between the two traditions is the way in which the Yajurvedic mantras are used in Vedic rituals. While the Krishna Yajurveda primarily relies on the chanting of the Veda mantras, the Shukla Yajurveda also includes some recitations of invocation and benediction which are unique to this Yajurvedic path.

Finally, the two Yajurvedic traditions also present distinct cosmological views. The Krishna Yajurveda presents a cyclic view of the universe, wherein creation occurs in cycles, each with its own separate beginning, middle and end. The Shukla Yajurveda, on the other hand, presents a linear view of time, wherein there is only one creation and no cycles of creation.

In conclusion, there are distinct differences between the Krishna and Shukla Yajurveda in terms of their physical compositions, ritual practises, and cosmological concepts. While both traditions follow the same ancient Vedic teachings, they provide unique perspectives on how to practice and understand these teachings. It is these differences that make the two traditions so appealing to so many people across the globe.

CHAPTER SIXTEEN

SHANKARACHARYA ON YAJURVEDA

Yajurveda is one of the oldest Vedic texts and one of the four most important books of the Hindu religion known as the 'Vedas'. It is considered to be the foundation of Vedic knowledge, and Shankaracharya is held in high regard as one of the greatest scholars to ever live in India. Shankaracharya dedicated his life to the study and teaching of Yajurveda and many of its teachings are still taught today.

Shankaracharya is the author of many commentaries on Yajurveda, including the celebrated Brahma Sutra. The Brahma Sutra is a collection of verses that explain the philosophy of Yajurveda. It is considered to be the most important commentary written on Yajurveda and it contains the core principles of Vedic thought. Shankaracharya's commentaries expound on the teachings of Yajurveda, elucidating its concepts, and also serve as a guide to attain the aim of life.

Shankaracharya's influence on Yajurveda is clear and undeniable. He is regarded as the single most important authority on Yajurveda and his renowned commentaries are held in the highest esteem. According to Shankaracharya, the purpose of Yajurveda is to cultivate inner peace and tranquility. He believes that one should strive to discover the truth and pay attention to the knowledge available in Yajurveda so that one's own knowledge can be enhanced. Moreover, Shankaracharya emphasizes that service to the people is included in the practice of Yajurveda as a part of Karma Yoga, which is the path of doing right deeds selflessly and living with the belief that one's work is enjoined with God's will. He states that everyone should adhere to the rules and regulations of Yajurveda and not indulge in any kind of unholy activities.

Shankaracharya has also written many commentaries on the Upanishads, the last part of Yajurveda that explains the Vedic doctrines. The Upanishads focus on the fundamental principles of Hinduism such as Atman (the Absolute) and Brahman (the Supreme Reality). Shankaracharya believes that the aim of life is to unify the individual consciousness with the cosmic consciousness, to attain moksha i.e. liberation. He stresses the importance of understanding Yajurveda and its principles to accomplish this goal.

In conclusion, Shankaracharya's commentaries on Yajurveda remain a treasured source of spiritual and philosophical wisdom to this day. His teachings are wise and help us to understand the Vedic principles in a deeper and more meaningful way. His commentaries are among the most important works in Hinduism and his teachings continue to guide the lives of many people throughout the world.

CHAPTER SEVENTEEN

VED VYASA AND YAJURVEDA

Vyasa and YajurVeda are two of the most prominent, recognizable, and important aspects of the Vedas, one of the sacred texts of Hinduism. Vyasa composed the entire text of the Vedas, and YajurVeda is a collection of rituals and mantras directly related to the earliest form of Hindu worship. Together, Vyasa and YajurVeda form a powerful foundation on which Hinduism stands, providing insight and guidance to its practitioners.

Vyasa is said to have composed the four Vedas, the oldest scriptures of Hinduism, by himself. The Vedas are the source of almost all the teaching of Hinduism and provide believers with the knowledge they need to lead fulfilling lives. Vyasa was also the author of the Mahabharata, one of the two major ancient Sanskrit epics, of which YajurVeda is a part.

YajurVeda is a collection of rituals, such as animal and human sacrifices, performed before gods and goddesses. These rituals were believed to bring blessings to an individual and the community, such as protection from illness and evil forces, success in battle, an increase in possessions, and the avoidance of disaster. The Yajurveda includes mantras, chants, and hymns written in Sanskrit that were used to remember and recite during the ritual-related ceremonies.

Today, YajurVeda is still widely used and respected as part of Hindu practice. These rituals are still practiced in Shrauta style, which is considered the ancient style of Hindu rituals from the Vedic period. Shrauta rituals rely heavily on YajurVeda, since its Sanskrit mantras, hymns, and chants are vital components of its practice. In the contemporary period, YajurVeda has been referred to as the Liturgy of the Mystics, a spiritual path that emphasizes personal transformation and understanding of the soul.

The Vedas and YajurVeda are important foundations of Hinduism and have greatly impacted the Indian culture and its beliefs. These ancient scriptures provide an invaluable source of knowledge and an understanding of the important roles that religion and beliefs have in our lives. Vyasa and YajurVeda have been revered for centuries and continue to be seen as essential parts of Hindu practice.

CHAPTER EIGHTEEN

DAYANANDA SARAWATI ON YAJURVEDA

Dayananda Saraswati, born in 1824, was an Indian religious reformer, who founded the Arya Samaji Movement and the Swami Dayananda Anglo-Vedic Educational Institute. He was an influential spiritual leader and scholar of the Hindu religion, dedicating his life to the revival of the Vedic knowledge and Sanatana Dharma. Dayananda is especially renowned for his commentary on Yajurveda, the fourth Veda in Hinduism.

Yajurveda is one of the four Vedic scriptures and it is a source of eternal wisdom. It contains various hymns, rituals and mantras to be used for the performance of Yajnas (sacrifices). Dayananda believed that Yajurveda contained truths that extend far beyond the comprehension of humans and was essential for spiritual growth and enlightenment. He devoted considerable energy to the interpretation of Yajurveda, understanding it as part of a timeless divine knowledge.

He was particularly drawn to Yajurveda because it dealt with the immortality of the soul. Dayananda believed that Yajurveda contained a wealth of information that could serve as a guide to self-realization and enlightenment. He maintained that Yajurveda exposed the truth of impermanence and the need to accept life as it comes. According to Dayananda, Yajurveda provides great insight into leading a life of balance, wisdom and non-attachment.

Dayananda was uncompromising in his interpretation of Yajurveda, often going against the grain of conventional Vedic practice. He recognized the need to adapt and update Hinduism to suit the changing needs of society; while still remaining true to its essence. He sought to expound a more fundamental and universally relevant interpretation of Yajurveda, seeking to draw out the deeper spiritual and philosophical truths that it contains. He maintained that through the comprehension of Yajurveda, one could gain a comprehensive insight into meditation, yoga, and other forms of spiritual practice.

Dayananda also believed that the deeper spiritual principles of Yajurveda could help to unite people of different castes and religions. His interpretations of Yajurveda aimed to promote a more equal, just and balanced society. Dayananda is also credited with producing one of the most complete texts on Vedic rituals and ceremonies, drawing his knowledge from Yajurveda.

In sum, Dayananda Saraswati's interpretation of Yajurveda helped to shed light on some of the deepest spiritual truths and make them accessible to a wider audience. He sought to promote balance, understanding and justice in society through his teachings on Yajurveda. Dayananda's legacy continues to this day, with many modern scholars attributing his work and insights as being a key influence in revitalizing Hinduism in the real understanding.

CHAPTER NINETEEN

KRISHNA YAJURVEDA

Krishna Yajurveda is one of the four Vedas of Hinduism. Known as the "Black Yajurveda", it is one of the oldest authoritative scriptures in the world and contains the knowledge of divine wisdom and advice for mundane matters. It is comprised of four major texts which are known as the Taittiriya, Kathaka, Shukla, andMaitrayani Samhitas.

The Taittiriya Samhita is the foundational text of the Yajurveda and is comprised of 36 chapters dealing with various rituals and ceremonies. This is then followed by the Kathaka Samhita which contains 60 sections of mantras and myths narrated by sage Krishna. Shukla Yajurveda constitutes the third samhita and is composed of 30 sections of verses arranged in three parts. Lastly, the Maitrayani Samhita includes the 84 chapters deliberating on rituals related to the sacrificial ceremonies.

From the samhitas, the mantras of Krishna Yajurveda are distinguished from other Vedas. These mantras are referred to by the Aryan gods, for instance Indra for mighty power and Mitra for friendship. Also, its mantras are categorized into different kinds based on their purpose and usage.

Some of it is used as blessings while some are used while conducting rituals or reciting mantras. Additionally, some of the mantras pertain to astronomy, like the Shukla Yajurveda's Piraskata mantra which explains the movements of the celestial bodies.

Besides mantras, the Yajurveda also covers the four different paths of truth – Samkhya, Yoga, Vaisesika, and Vedanta. These paths pertain to the practice of physical postures like asana and pranayama, meditation, and spiritual knowledge. This practice is known as Shakta which means "with power", and helps to bring the practitioner closer in contact with the divine.

In addition to the four paths of teachings and mantras, the Yajurveda also continually highlights the importance of ethics and dharma. In this, it encourages the practitioners to consider the effects of their actions, sacrifice for the benefit of others, and selflessly help anyone who is in need.

All in all, Krishna Yajurveda is a comprehensive collection of spiritual and secular wisdom. It is a rich source of knowledge and provides invaluable insights on the essence of life, uncovering a deeper understanding of the roots of Hinduism. As it delves into the rituals and practices, mantras, and paths of knowledge, the Krishna Yajurveda offers great insight and understanding into spiritual insight and ultimate truth.

CHAPTER TWENTY

SHUKLA YAJURVEDA

Shukla Yajurveda is an ancient traditional Hindu scripture that predates the 6th century BCE. It is preserved in several of the oldest Indian texts and is one of the oldest known religious texts in the world. The Yajurveda is comprised of four distinct Vedas: the Rig Veda, the Sama Veda, the Atharva Veda, and the Shukla Yajurveda.

The Shukla Yajurveda is focused primarily on rituals and worship and contains the largest collection of Mantras, or hymns, of any of the Vedas. However, it is more than just these religious elements; it is a philosophical exploration of the relationship between man and the divine, taking a deeper look at concepts such as karma, atman, and dharma. The book also contains offerings to gods, detailing the ritualistic nature of ancient Hinduism and providing detailed instructions for said rituals.

Shukla Yajurveda is divided into two parts: the White Yajurveda and the Black Yajurveda. The former is further divided into two Brahmanas and four Upanishads—brief, philosophical encounters between a teacher and student. The latter is further subdivided into two Samhitas—an elaborate liturgy composed of hymns and mantras.

The text of the Shukla Yajurveda is dense, verbose, and demanding, requiring focus and dedication to understand. It contains copious information, not just on rituals and prayers, but on the laws of sacrifice (yajnas), the use of certain sacred objects, and even festivals and events. Furthermore, it contains stories and detail around Hindu gods and mythology, including descriptions of their appearance and abilities.

The Shukla Yajurveda has been profoundly influential in India and the wider Hindu diaspora, influencing the beliefs of many practitioners and giving shape to their worship. Indeed, even today much of Indian culture, such as Hindu bachelor and master-level rituals, direct their scripts and procedures from the ancient Shukla Yajurveda traditions.

To conclude, Shukla Yajurveda is an ancient and sacred Hindu scripture, dating back several centuries BCE and containing a wealth of important information about Hinduism and its rituals. It has been immensely influential in the centuries since its inception, providing practitioners and scholars alike with insights into the philosophical, religious, and ritualistic aspects of Indian culture.

CHAPTER TWENTY-ONE

SUMMARY

Yajurveda, one of the four sacred texts of the Vedic religion, is an ancient religious and philosophical text. The text is traditionally divided into two sections: the Samhitas, which is composed of prose mantras and rituals, and the Brahmanas, which contain traditional commentaries and explanations of Hindu beliefs and rituals.

The Samhita is the first main division of the Yajurveda. It is divided into four books, each focusing on different aspects of Hindu mythology and philosophy. The foremost of these books is the Shukla Yajurveda, which contains a collection of prayers, hymns, and sacrifices associated with various Hindu deities. This book is considered to be the source of the sacrificial ritual known as the Yajna. Another important book is the Krishna Yajurveda, which focuses on the philosophy of Vedic rituals and serves as a source of commentaries on the Shukla Yajurveda.

The Brahmanas comprise the second main division of the Yajurveda. This section contains traditional commentaries and explanations of Hindu beliefs and rituals. These commentaries usually include an analysis of Vedic texts and their application in everyday life. Notable examples include the Aitareya Brahmana, which provides an explanation of sacrificial ritual, the Jaiminiya Brahmana, which offers guidance concerning the invocation of gods, and the Taittiriya Brahmana, which provides an insight into the doctrine of transmigration.

The Yajurveda has long been seen as a source of spiritual, religious, and philosophical knowledge. It is revered by many Hindus as one of the four most ancient and sacred texts in the Vedic religion. Its contents have served as an important source of inspiration and understanding of the Hindu religion and its various rituals and beliefs. For this reason, the Yajurveda remains a vital source of Hindu knowledge and study.

Contact

DR. JAGADEESH PILLAI

PhD in Vedic Science

Four Times Guinness World Record Holder

Winner of Mahatma Gandhi Vishwa Shanti Puraskar and Global Peace Ambassador

9839093003

myrichindia@gmail.com

drjagadeeshpillai@facebook

drjagadeeshpillai@instagram

jagadeeshpillai@youtube

www. JAGADEESHPILLAI.com

Author's Other Books

1. The Moments When I Met God
2. Kashiyile Theertha Pathangal
3. GURU GYAN VANI
4. Abhiprerak Gita
5. ASSI SE JAIN GHAT TAK
6. Hopelessness of Arjuna
7. The Soul and It's True Nature
8. Sense of Action (Karma)
9. Action through Wisdom
10. Action through Wisdom
11. THEORY AND PRACTICAL OF EVERY ACTION
12. LOGICAL UNDERSTANDING OF THE SUPREME
13. THE IMPERISHABLE SUPREME
14. Yatra Nishadraj se Hanuman Ghat Tak
15. Yatra Karnatak Ghat se Raja Ghat Tak
16. Yatra Pandey Ghat se Prayagraj Ghat Tak
17. Yatra Ranjendra Prasad Ghat se Dattatreya Ghat Tak
18. YaatraSindhiya Ghat se Gwaliar Ghat Tak
19. Yatra Mangala Gauri Ghat se Hanuman Gadhi Ghat Tak
20. Yatra Gaay Ghat Se Nishad Ghat Tak
21. MAA GANGA, GHATEN EVM UTSAV
22. Ganga Arti Dev Deepavali evam Any Utsav
23. Potentials of Digitalized India
24. VEDIC CONSCIOUSNESS
25. A Brief Introduction to Vedic Science
26. Kashi ke Barah Jyotirling
27. IMPACT OF MOTIVATION
28. Let's have a Milky Way Journey
29. Color Therapy in a Nutshell

30. Rigveda in a Nutshell
31. Yajurveda in a Nutshell
32. Samveda in a Nutshell
33. Atharva Veda in a Nutshell
34. Ayurveda in a Nutshell
35. Srimad Bhagavad Gita and Upanishad Connection

9 798889 093701

Printed by Libri Plureos GmbH in Hamburg, Germany